2014

Create your Amazing... Year

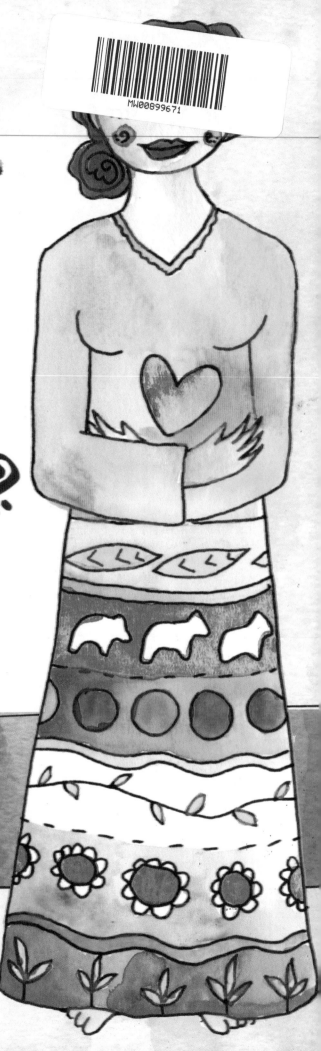

LIFE + BIZ EDITION
WORKBOOK

Leonie Dawson

DEDICATED TO:
Every Woman. You each deserve incredible,
beautiful lives that sing to your soul.

WORLD CHANGING PHILANTHROPY:
A portion of profits from every workbook will go
to a range of charities that support the world to
become an even better place.

WARNING!

THIS WORKBOOK CREATES CHANGE

Five years ago, I did a crazy little creative side project to plan out my new year. It ended up going out into the world and becoming an instant hit. Not only that, it started making miracles. Changing lives. Making dreams happen. Every single year since then, thousands of women have created their own amazing year, life + business using this workbook.

This special life + business edition will guide you through the specific process of planning out and growing your most amazing year yet.

In life, this workbook will help you cultivate the kind of joy, peace and fulfilment you've been seeking. You'll see some of your biggest dreams come to life.

In business, it will help you plan out your best year yet. This workbook is part of the work I use with my private coaching business clients (+ in my own high six figure business) to catapult them into incredible success. When used + implemented, this workbook has the potential to double or triple your business. These questions are powerful + profound changemakers that will help you see just where your business is at, what it needs + how to get it to where you want to go.

Miracles happen when you get this kind of clarity.

Ready for the ginormous, glorious change that is coming?

Your amazing year in life + business is waiting.

about Leonie Dawson.

Leonie Dawson is a mentor to women wanting to create incredible businesses + lives. She is also an author, retreat leader, visual artist, mama and guide for the tens of thousands who receive her free "AMAZING BIZ + LIFE" ezine each week.

Leonie is a successful entrepreneur who has created a half million dollar a year company that helps thousands of women every single year. Her mission is to help as many earth angels – women with creative or spiritual gifts – to have profoundly profitable businesses so they may nourish themselves and heal the world.

Leonie has taught alongside such luminaries as Arielle Ford, Julia Cameron, Gay Hendricks and SARK. Leonie has coached tens of thousands of women to create their own incredible businesses + lives including crystal healers, celebrities, coaches, best-selling authors, award-winning singers, fitness experts, yoga teachers, multiple-six-figure entrepreneurs and artists.

Her strategic musings and practical wisdom have been featured on Problogger, Tiny Buddha, magazines like Spellcraft, Life Images, Goddess and Spheres, and in three of SARK's best-selling books on creative fulfillment & freedom.

Leonie has also worked as editor of the Australian Government's business website business.gov.au which garnered a United Nations award.

Best-selling author of "Succulent Wild Woman" SARK has called Leonie "a gifted goddess and illuminated creator. I happily recommend her and her lilting work." Hay House author of "Oracle Tarot", Lucy Cavendish has said "Leonie Dawson is an amazing artist and spiritual teacher. She's inspiring, wise, kind and oh-so-talented."

LET'S GET CONNECTED ON WWW.LEONIEDAWSON.COM

I've been featured in

zenhabits : breathe

canberratimes.com.au
The Canberra Times

THE HUFFINGTON POST

G'day Amazing Woman

Congratulations on taking this time now to create your year ahead. We all have resolutions, wishes + dreams to create an amazing life for ourselves. Amazing years don't happen by chance however.

We are the ones who need to make it happen. We need to vision it, dream it, map it out, plan it and MAKE IT HAPPEN.

This workbook will guide you through the doing of just that. This workbook is a major miracle maker - not just in my life but for the thousands of women who have been using this book for 5 years now.

Let's go create your AMAZING 2014 NOW!

Leonie Dawson

2014

Create your Amazing... Year

LIFE EDITION
WORKBOOK

Leonie Dawson

Ideas for using this planner

 Fill it all out or just the parts that sing to you (either is perfect)

 Make sure you put it in your calendar to review your workbook regularly to keep you on track - I do it monthly with myself, and quarterly with my team. The more you review it, the more of your goals will come true! Check out my video on creating your own scrap journal!

www.LeonieDawson.com/scrap-journal

 Put the pages that most sing to you on your wall or pin board to remind you during your year

 Put your goals into your to do list or calendar

 Add to it as your year blooms

 Share it publicly or semi-privately with accountability partners or your mastermind group to get publicly accountable... that stuff is dang motivating!

IMPORTANT REMINDER: There is no right or wrong way. There are no obligations or requirements. Whatever feels joyful, easy, gorgeous & good for you is perfect ♡ A+++

THE VERY IMPORTANT

2013

Closing Ceremony

Celebrating & Releasing 2013

Here's the place where we muck it up.

We set our NEW resolutions, our NEW goals, our NEW dreams... without ever taking stock, coming to terms with and clearing all the days and months that have gone before us.

It is so deeply important for us to find the gifts, medicine, lessons, challenges and blessings from the year that has been. Only in doing this celebration and release of the year will we find peace and clarity.

During our closing ceremony over the next few pages, you will begin to see your life with clear, bright eyes. You will find the understanding you've been seeking. From the tangled ball of threads, a rich tapestry will emerge. And it will be more beautiful, deep and profound than you could possibly imagine.

You've been sent here on a mission. To discover every part of your self. To grow wiser than you ever thought possible. To find the light even in the darkest cave.

2013 happened to you the way it did for a reason. Sometimes they are reasons you cannot possibly begin to know right now. At other times the reason + the blessing is easy to see. Even when it's hard, it doesn't mean it wasn't meant to happen. It's all taking you to where you need to go.

You are getting braver, deeper, wiser, more beautiful by the moment, by the day, by the year.

Let's celebrate + release 2013. And clear the pathway for the miracles to come.

She chose love, not fear, and that made all the difference.

Celebrating & Releasing 2013

 What beautiful lessons did you learn during 2013?

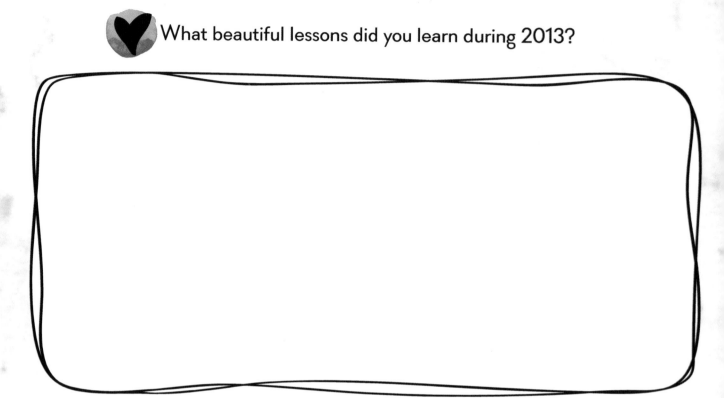 What dreams came true during 2013?

Celebrating & Releasing 2013

I know myself now more because...

I was transformed this year by...

I let go of...

I am happy because of...

Celebrating & Releasing 2013

⭐ The incredible thing I discovered about myself was...

🍃 2013 led me to...

🌹 I am proud of myself for...

Celebrating & Releasing 2013

What do you need to share/rant/journal/express/write about to feel COMPLETE about 2013? Do it here.

Celebrating & Releasing 2013

A page of gratitude. Draw, write, illustrate, post pictures of
EVERYTHING you are grateful for from 2013

COMPLETION CIRCLE

(place your hand in the circle to recieve the energy)

We breath & give thanks for all that has passed...

We open up to the beautiful possibilities blossoming before us...

We let go & breathe releasing all that is old & no longer serves us...

We radiate in light & joy...all is beautiful & all is well...

2014

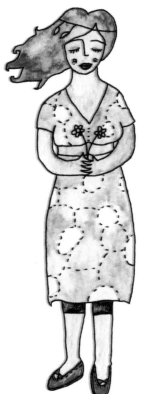

It's time to dream a new dream.

Time to create an incredible year for yourself, your world, the world.

First comes the THOUGHT

Then the WORD

Then the ACTION.

That's how change happens.

Are you Ready?

[ ] YES   [ ] NO

Invoking 2014

 Darlingheart, what do you most want to experience 2014 as?

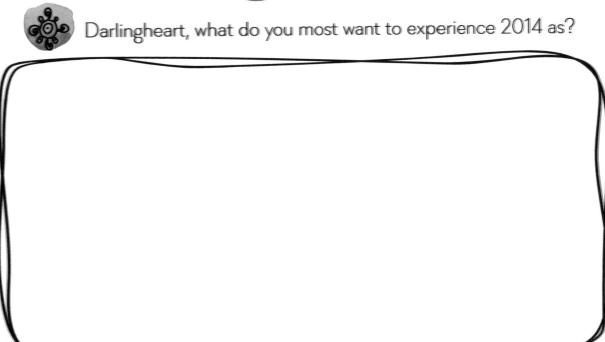

What do you want to feel during 2014?

Invoking 2014

 What do you want to give yourself in 2014?

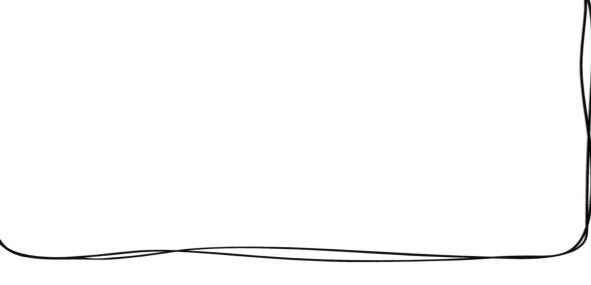

How would you like to donate time or money to change the world this year?

THIS YEAR, I GIVE MYSELF PERMISSION TO...

This year I promise to myself that I will...

2014 will be the year that...

100 Things to Do in 2014

1.
2.
3.
4.
5.
6.
7.
8.
9.
10.
11.
12.
13.
14.
15.
16.
17.
18.
19.

20.
21.
22.
23.
24.
25.
26.
27.
28.
29.
30.
31.
32.
33.
34.
35.
36.

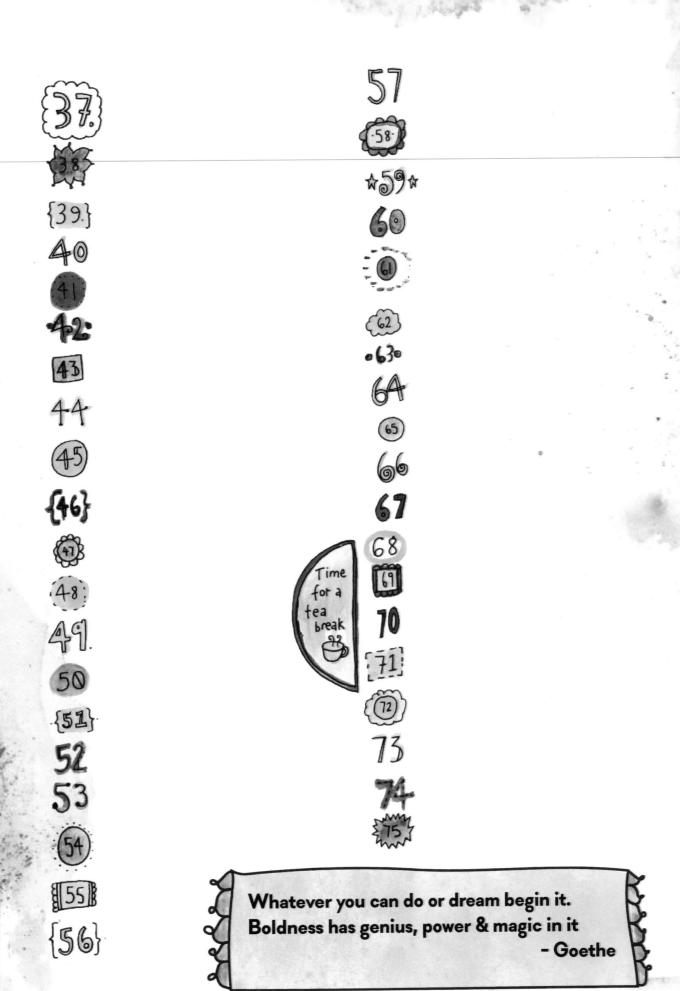

37. 38 {39.} 40 41 42 43 44 45 {46} 47 48 49 50 {51} 52 53 54 55 {56}

57 58 59 60 61 62 63 64 65 66 67 68 69 70 71 72 73 74 75

Time for a tea break

Whatever you can do or dream begin it. Boldness has genius, power & magic in it
- Goethe

76
77
78
79
80
81
{82}
83
84
·85·
86
86
[87]
88.
89
90
91
92.
93
{94}

95
96
97.
98.
99
100

Goddess of New Beginnings

Begin again.
Pick up your
cape & your
walking stick.
Weave a soft
basket for all
your dreams.
Take a deep
breath & set
your eyes to the
horizon.
You are the
goddess of
New
beginnings. anything
is possible....

~Leonie

The List of Things To Do When Everything Sucks

(you can read more about this at www.LeonieDawson.com/Everything-sucks)

Our feelings can change in an instant. Fickle things they are - generated by the moment, the situation, our hormones & our perspective. If we can change just one of these things, a great healing can occur.

We can go from rock bottom to "you know what? I'm okay..." in about 15 minutes. There's a world of difference between those 2 places. All we need to do is remember the things that work for us...the little changes that can make a big difference.

Let's prepare ourselves now...write our reminder list of Things To Do When Everything Sucks.

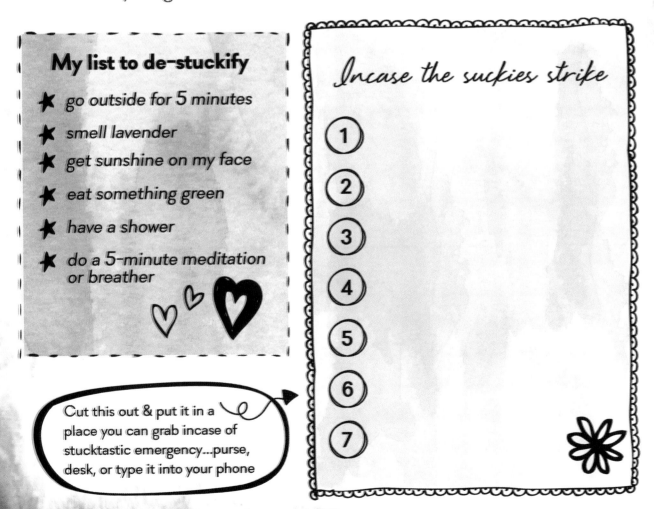

My list to de-stuckify

★ go outside for 5 minutes

★ smell lavender

★ get sunshine on my face

★ eat something green

★ have a shower

★ do a 5-minute meditation or breather

Cut this out & put it in a place you can grab incase of stucktastic emergency...purse, desk, or type it into your phone

Incase the suckies strike

1
2
3
4
5
6
7

Affirmations

Create your own.
Collage. Cut out.
Put around your
home, in your diary,
pockets & purse

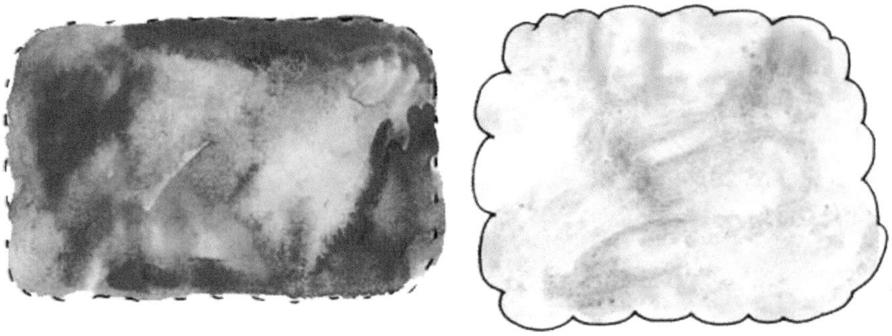

YOU ARE ★ RADIANT

you are loved ♥

Ritual Days

We all know we need to do things that fill us up...it's just hard to remember to fit-it-in sometimes...

Here's where RITUAL DAYS come in handy!

What are all the things you want to do weekly? Turn them into days!

You could have...

ADVENTURE saturDays

switch off suNDays

SpA thursdays

Artist Date mondays...

go-To-Bed -Early WEDNESDAYS

HeaLing FRIDAYS

CREative TuesDay...

WHAT DO YOU NEED TO GIVE YOURSELF?

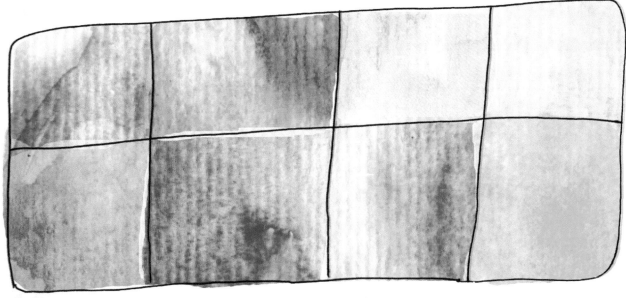

(Then pop on your calendar!)

This year, I want to give myself the gift of...

This year, what would I like to release?

my Amazing goals 2014

Ack! I know right? Making New Year's goals can be scary - sometimes they remind us of the goals we've made before that haven't come true yet.

Have no fear though gorgeous soul. Together we will dream big AND make those dreams possible & practical, so you know just what to do next.

FYI: These questions are POWERFUL & they WILL create change in your life. The kind of change you've been dreaming about.

Just follow the worksheets & I'll guide you joyfully along the journey of making your AMAZING DREAMS COME TRUE!

First your task is to DREAM BIG & start writing those dreams down

my Amazing goals 2014

 My financial goals are...

My gorgeous goddess body goals are...

my Amazing goals 2014

My business or work goals are...

My creative goals are...

my Amazing goals 2014

 My spiritual goals are...

 My family & friendship goals are...

my Amazing goals 2014

 My personal goals are...

My goals that are so big & daring that I'm not even sure they are possible are...

HURRAH! YOU DREAMED BIG!

You can always go back & add to it later...

NEXT STEP...

The next step to make now that you've dreamed big is to make your goals possible & practical.

You need to create a TO DO LIST BOOK.

You can see a video of mine & pictures of other goddess books by going to:

http://tinyurl.com/todobook

All you need is a book you can write in - it can be any size you like. Lined or unlined. One where you can tear pages out is good. You can decorate it or keep it plain. You can call it your To Do List book or you can call it a BOOK OF MAGNIFICENT POSSIBILITIES!

YOU CAN CALL IT YOUR GODDESS GUIDE...

... or you can call it your book of making dreams come true.

Whatever makes you light up is perfect!

And now you've got your To Do List book? YAY!

At the top of each page in your book, write down each of your goals.

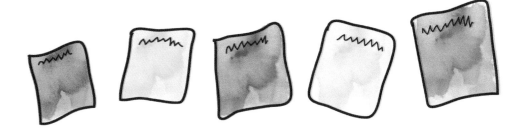

Then, under each of your goals, start writing down ways to make this happen & all the steps you need to take.

Use this shorthand way of marking out possibilities & steps....

For example...

GO TO HAWAII

⊗ ? Maybe July while on break

? Maybe with goddess sisters?

Ⓐ Research cheapest flights [next week]

Ⓐ Create a Hawaii dreamboard [SUNDAY]

Ⓐ Work out budget for it [Tuesday]

Ⓐ Dream up ways to earn extra money for Hawaii fund

? for possibilites & ideas

Ⓐ For every item that is actionable

Put a timeline for actionable items in a box beside it.

The Ⓐ items are your key to making your gorgeous goddess goal happen.

Divide up your goals into actionable items, things you can begin doing right now.

Add a time next to your Ⓐ items for a date to make it happen.

If you are finding it hard to get started on an Ⓐ item, break it up into even smaler Ⓐ items & mini steps.

Make it easy, joyful & doable for you ♡

(You can then add your items into your diary on their days of doing if you like)

You don't have to write down all the Ⓐ items to get you to your goal right now if that feels overwhelming.

Just pop down the ones you can start thinking about & doing right now.

Then once you've completed them you can add the next steps.

Go for it gorgeous goddess & creat your To Do List book.

It will become the blueprint for making your goals & dreams come true in 2014 for you.

Ⓐ. Create your To Do list book

Ⓐ. Make your goals Actionable.

My Mottos

For an easy way to remember what you are trying to cultivate, create some gorgeous goddess mottos.

Here's some examples of mottos for making a magnificent year.

My Mottos

You are amazing, just as you are...

TEN THINGS I WANT TO CELEBRATE ABOUT MYSELF IN 2014

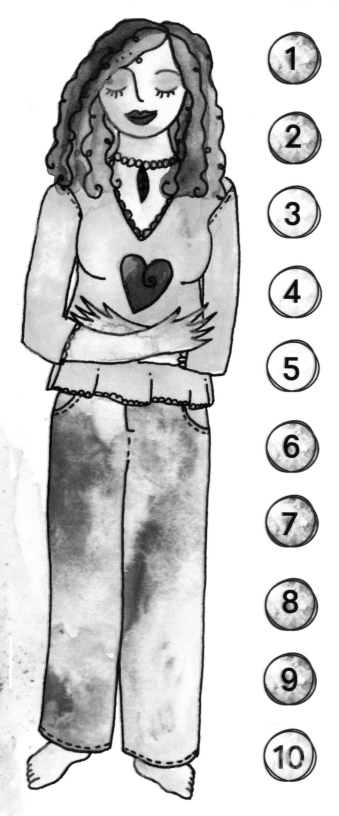

1

2

3

4

5

6

7

8

9

10

2014 AN IMMERSED IN LOVE PORTRAIT

Paste a photo of yourself in the bordered frame...and then all around the photo, write love letters, reminders, messages of support...all the things you need to hear. During the year you'll be able to look back & feel all the love & soul reminders again.

WHAT I'D LIKE TO LEARN IN 2014...

What teachers & mentors would I like to invite into my life?

HOW WOULD YOU LIKE TO CELEBRATE YOUR BIRTHING DAY THIS YEAR?

CREATE YOUR OWN

my Amazing Habits LIST

What joyful, nourishing & centering habits would you like to cultivate during 2014? Don't worry about how hard it is to form habits - what we'll be doing instead is creating a poster to remind ourselves each day of the beautiful things we'd like to do.

Somedays we might do all of them, most days we'll only get to some...other days we may not get to any of them. All of this is gorgeous & fine.

It's not about perfection or failure. What it's about is reminding ourselves of the sacred toolkit of activities we have available to us.

Brainstorm what goddess habits you'd like to include & create your own poster. I've included a blank one you can fill out & two examples you can draw inspiration from. You can do it!

THINGS TO THINK ABOUT WHEN CREATING YOUR
my Amazing Habits

 Make them sound like fun. Use words that lift you & get you excited to do it..

 Make your habits feel achievable. On my list I say to move for five minutes – even though I almost always do way more. If I wrote it down as moving for 15 minutes, it would sound like too much for me & I would avoid it like crazy. Make it achievable so when you do get it done, you'll feel that gorgeous sense of HURRAH & will continue on making habits happen in your day. Any extra you do will be a bountiful bonus.

 Phrase them positively as something to move towards instead of being a "Don't."

 Copy habits that sing to you & listen to your spirit to hear what it needs.

There is a wise woman in you who knows the way.

12 ZEN HABITS

1 — Set your 3 MITSs (most important tasts) each morning

2 — Single-task (focus your attention)

3 — Zero inbox

4 — Process emails once a day

5 — Exercise 5-10 mins a day

6 — Work while disconnected

7 — Keep your desk decluttered

8 — Clear & declutter home for 15 minutes a day

9 — Stick to a 5 sentence limit on emails (make your words powerful)

10 — Say no to commitments & requests not on your importance short list

11 — Eat fresh fruit & veg everyday

12 — Follow a morning routine

From Leo Babauta at www.zenhabits.net

LEONIE'S HABITS THAT MAKE HER SHINE

1. Set your 3 Most Important Tasks & intentions for your day in the morning

2. Meditate however you like

3. Divine declutter & make one area feel clear, cozy & gorgeous ★

4. Move your body for at least five minutes...

5. Eat fruit & vege that make you feel radiant & gorgeous...

6. Ground outside

7. give thanks

8. Be joyful, positive & impeccable with your word

9. Switch off to focus

10. Switch off at least 30 mins before bed

my Amazing Habits

How I Currently Spend My Time

Create a pie chart of how you spend your time...

How I Want to Spend My Time

Word for the Year

If you could pick a goddess theme as a power word,
or affirmation of what you'd like to experience &
focus on for your year, what would it be?

MY SACRED WORD FOR 2014 IS...

BONUS, OPTIONAL, EXTRA ACTIVITY

Create a collage or artwork
with your sacred word on it so
you can see & remember &
embrace your theme everyday.
For more on this project go to...

www.LeonieDawson.com/Word-Year

LET'S SUPERCHARGE YOUR WORD OF THE YEAR!

Sometimes it's not enough just to make up your theme for the year. You need to go deeper. Work out what's in alignment with your word and what's not. Then your year will start feeling so much more like the way you want it too!

Consider your word of the year. What currently DOESN'T feel like that in your life? What activities, times of the day, relationships, habits, emotions don't resonate with it?

What would bring more of that quality into your life?

BRAINSTORM ALL YOUR ACTIONABLES FOR MAKING YOUR WORD HAPPEN.

How can you stop or transform the things that don't resonate with your word?

How can you do more of the things that do?

DESCRIBE YOUR DREAMIEST DAY THAT YOU WOULD ♥LOVE♥ TO HAPPEN THIS YEAR

BOOKS I'D LIKE TO READ...

PLACES I'D ♥ TO VISIT...

WHAT DO YOU WANT TO STOP DOING THIS YEAR?

HOW WOULD I LIKE MY HOME TO FEEL THIS YEAR?

WHAT ARE 5 WAYS I CAN HELP MY HOME FEEL LIKE THIS?

Retreat

Plan a CREATIVE & SOULFUL retreat for yourself this year.

WHEN? ♥ ♥ ♥ ♥

HOW LONG?

WHERE?

WHAT WILL YOU DO?

Now schedule it in! Put it in the calendar! Plan now to make it happen!

HOW MY BODY FEELS
RIGHT NOW

Color in. Collage. Fill with words...

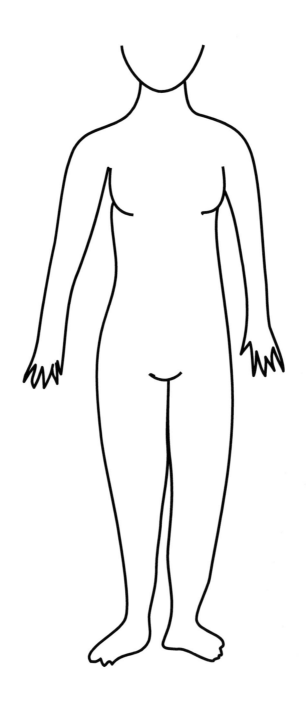

HOW I'D LIKE MY BODY
TO FEEL THIS YEAR...

Color in. Collage. Fill with words...

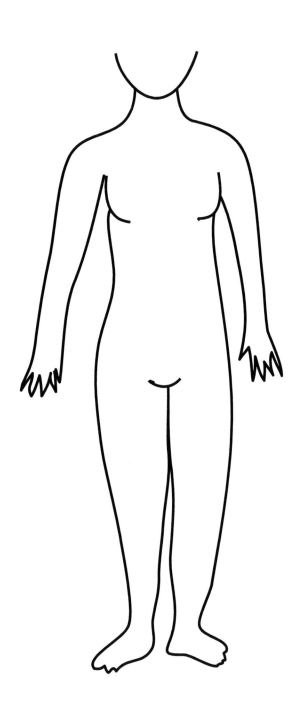

PEOPLE I'D LOVE TO SPEND TIME WITH OR CONNECT WITH THIS YEAR...

MOVIES, CONCERTS OR SHOWS I'D LOVE TO SEE THIS YEAR...

If you can't think of specific ones, write & describe an imaginary one - what it includes & how it makes you feel...

CREATING YOUR MEDICINE BAG OF TOOLS

What tools can you turn to when you need extra energy or a reminder that you are a goddess? i.e. friends, books, self-comfort, activities, healing tools, centering practices.

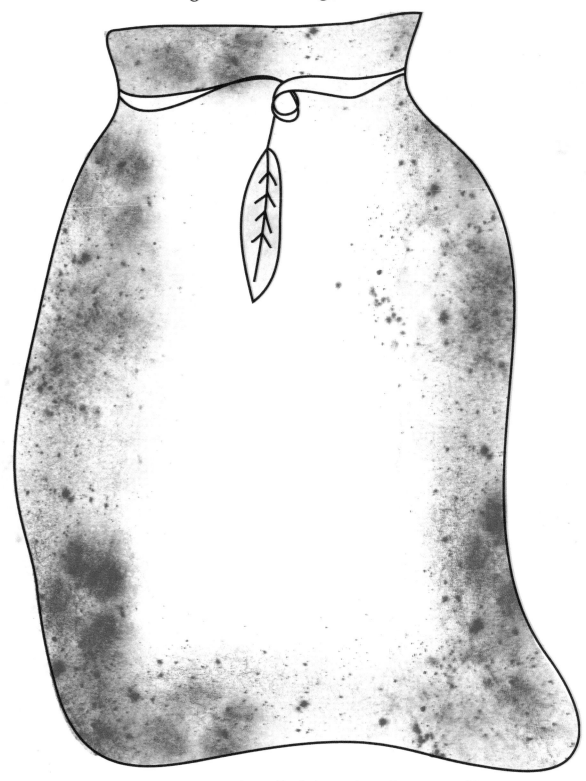

CREATE A Dreamboard FOR 2014

Dreamboards are an incredibly powerful tool for drawing your dreams to you through the Law of Attraction. Not only that, they serve as visual guideposts that are not only beautiful and inspiring to look at, but will help you remember every.single.day of your dreams + highest intentions for this year.

And as we all know, what we focus on becomes true. Creating your very own dreamboard right now will help seal the deal between you and your dreams!

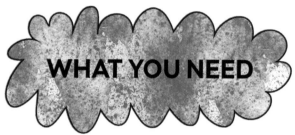

WHAT YOU NEED

 A PIECE OF CARDBOARD, THICK PAPER OR CANVAS IN WHATEVER SIZE FEELS RIGHT TO YOU.

 MAGAZINES, NEWSPAPERS, PHOTOS, IMAGES & WORDS.

 GLUE.

 A LITTLE BLEND OF OPENESS, COURAGE, JOY & A SPRINKLE OF HOPE.

 TOP WITH ESSENCE OF BIG DREAMS.

CREATE A Dreamboard FOR 2014

AND NOW...

 Search through the magazines, etc. for images & words of all the things you'd like to draw into your life experience & feel during your year.

 Choose images & words that lift you up, inspire you and make you feel radiant. Ignore all images & words that feel like a "should."

 Paste them onto your cardboard until it feels just right for your gorgeous spirit.

 Put it in a place where you can see it when you fall asleep & as you wake up.

 Watch as it is all drawn magically into your life...

Dream Board EXAMPLES

WANT TO
WATCH A VIDEO
NOW TOO?

www.LeonieDawson.com/Dreamboard

CUT OUT PICTURES OR DRAW THE THINGS YOU WANT TO INVITE INTO YOUR LIFE THIS YEAR

(Experiences, adventures, relationships, possesions, things...)

GIVE YOURSELF ONE

Oracle Card Reading

FOR THE YEAR

 Pull 12 oracle or tarot cards for your year ahead....

 Ask your angels & guides what you need to know to help you glow

 If you don't have your own cards, try an online oracle... I ♥ Joanna Powell Colbert at www.gaiantarot.com

 Write down the card messages for each month...just go with the words that feel the most important.

2014 Oracle Reading

I used Lucy Cavendish's "Oracle of the Dragonfae" for my reading.

They are my favorite cards to do readings with - they have become like dear friends to me!

www.tinyurl.com/dragonfaecards

There are so many oracle & tarot cards out there that you can use. Choose the one that calls to your heart.

For a list of some of my other favourite oracle cards, head to:

www.tinyurl.com/top5oracle

I began giving myself "yearly forecast" oracle readings in 2011.

I just began by scrawling down the themes on a piece of paper.

It amazed me as I referred back to it each month how accurate & helpful it had been.

And it was so beautiful & useful when it came to preparing for what was to come to!

my 2011 card reading... amazingly accurate

2014 Oracle Reading

January

February

March

April

May

June

2014 Oracle Reading

July

August

September

October

November

December

GET YOUR BONUS 2014 CREATE YOUR AMAZING YEAR IN LIFE CALENDAR!

Just for being a workbook goddess, I want to give you a free matching gift... the official 2014 Create Your Amazing Year Life calendar!

Head to: www.leoniedawson.com/bonus2014

to get your FREE BONUS calendar now!

2014

Create your Amazing... Year

BIZ EDITION
WORKBOOK

Leonie Dawson

g'day Amazing Woman!

CONGRATULATIONS!

Business doesn't have to be hard. It doesn't have to break your finances, your life balance or your spirit. It can be enormously joyful, profitable and help thousands of people. It can be a living embodiment of spirit. You CAN have time off. You CAN make glorious amounts of abundance. You CAN live your soul purpose.

What do you need to do to make it happen? You need to dedicate yourself to this work. To dreaming your biggest dream. To becoming the person you need to become in order to make them happen. To the work of growing and evolving and learning. To making maximum impact (without giving up your life or family to do it.) To investing in you & your dreams.

But I gotta tell you a secret I've learned over the years of helping women create incredible lives + incredible businesses:

NOT EVERYONE IS READY TO DO THIS WORK.

But just the mere fact that you've invested in this workbook sets you apart.

This workbook is going to take you through the essential questions you need to answer in order to shift your business (and life) into something incredible over the next year. I know it works, because I've been using the same questions to double or triple my business every single year. And all while working just a couple of hours a day. My priority is always on hanging out with my beautiful family, and living my biggest life. My business just happens to be my most favourite passion and hobby that fuels it all.

This can be your life too.

Are you ready to be incredible?

THE VERY IMPORTANT

2013

Closing Ceremony

Celebrating & Releasing 2013

What are your business accomplishments over the past year?

(Fill a page - they can be big or small! They are ALL important!)

Celebrating & Releasing 2013

What beautiful lessons did you learn during 2013?

What dreams came true during 2013?

Celebrating & Releasing 2013

What were your weak points?
What do you know needs to improve?

Celebrating & Releasing 2013

Do you have employees or contractors you work with?
How did your relationship with them this year pan out?
How could you improve your working relationship with them?

What challenges and blessings did you have with customer service this year?
How could you improve your customer service?

Celebrating & Releasing 2013

What were the areas that felt out of whack, hard to follow
or crazy-making this year?
What could be done to change them?

Celebrating & Releasing 2013

Okay. Are you ready love? It's time to take a look at MONEY.

We often avoid looking at real figures – and yet it is tremendously powerful for us to know our numbers so we can GROW them. You can do this, love. (This page will earn you more money than any other.) Yes, it really IS that important & powerful!

What was your gross profit for 2013?
(i.e. What was the total amount of money that came into the business?)

What were your total expenses for 2013?

What was your net profit for 2013 (i.e. total income minus expenses)?

IMPORTANT NOTE: DO NOT GET DISCOURAGED BY THESE NUMBERS. THEY ARE NOT THE NUMERIC VALUE OF YOUR WORTH OR DREAM. THEY ARE JUST NUMBERS. NUMBERS THAT CAN GROW AS SOON AS WE KNOW WHERE WE ARE GROWING FROM!

Celebrating & Releasing 2013

What were your five biggest selling products or services this year?

Rank them in order. And if you can add how much each one earnt too, you'll get a hundred million bonus points (AND it will give you a butt-load more of clarity AND make you a shit-tonne more moolah!)

1.

2.

3.

4.

5.

How big is your mailing list? How much did it increase in 2013?

How many Twitter followers or Facebook fans do you have (or pick the social media network of your choice)? How much did those numbers increase in 2013?

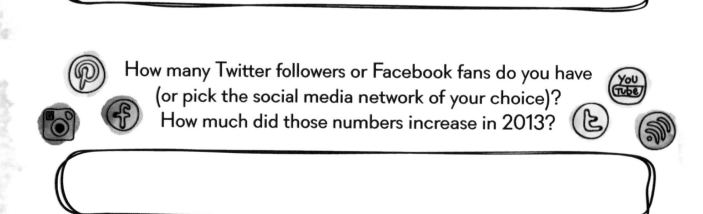

Celebrating & Releasing 2013

What marketing WORKED for you this year? What created wins for you?

How many days off did you take in the last year?

Do you want to donate time or money this year?
Who do you want to help and how?

What was the worst thing about your business in 2013?

What was the best thing about your business in 2013?

Celebrating & Releasing 2013

What do you need to write/journal/rant about/express in order for you to feel clear about 2013 in your business + life?

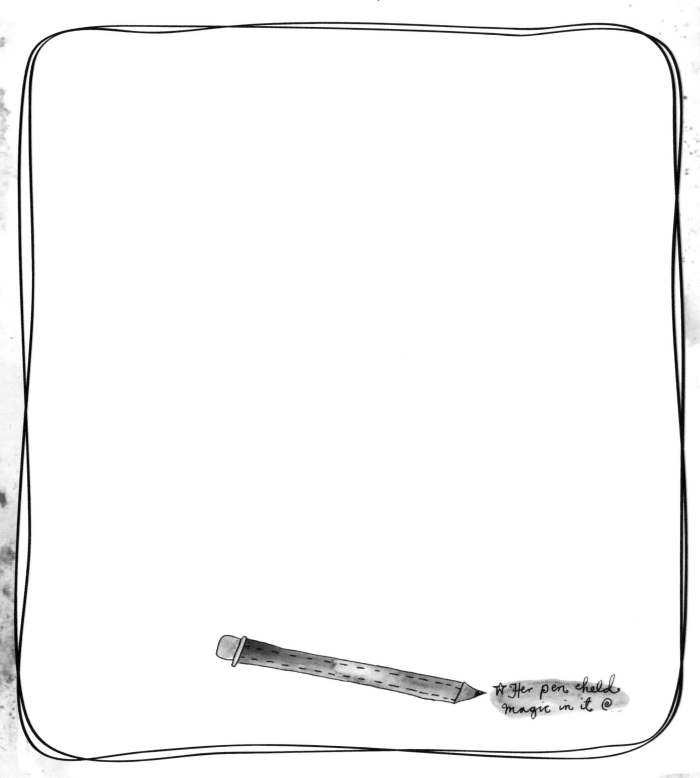

☆ Her pen held magic in it ☺

Celebrating & Releasing 2013

A page of gratitude. Draw, write, illustrate, post pictures of
EVERYTHING you are grateful for in your business world from 2013

COMPLETION CIRCLE

(place your hand in the circle to recieve the energy)

We breath & give thanks for all that has passed...

We open up to the beautiful possibilities blossoming before us...

We let go & breathe releasing all that is old & no longer serves us...

We radiate in light & joy...all is beautiful & all is well...

2014

It's time to dream a new dream for your business.

Time to create an incredible year for yourself, your world, the world.

First comes the THOUGHT

Then the WORD

Then the ACTION.

That's how change happens.

are you Ready?

☐ YES ☐ NO

Invoking MY 2014 BUSINESS

What does my 2014 business look like?

THIS YEAR, I GIVE MYSELF PERMISSION TO...

This year I promise to myself that I will...

2014 will be the year that...

my Amazing goals 2014

Ack! I know right? Making New Year's goals can be scary - sometimes they remind us of the goals we've made before that haven't come true yet.

Have no fear though gorgeous soul. Together we will dream big AND make those dreams possible & practical, so you know just what to do next.

FYI: These questions are POWERFUL & they WILL create change in your life. The kind of change you've been dreaming about.

Just follow the worksheets & I'll guide you joyfully along the journey of making your AMAZING BUSINESS DREAMS COME TRUE!

First your task is to DREAM BIG & start writing those dreams down

my Amazing goals 2014

 What are your income goals for 2014?

How will you achieve this? How many products/services will you sell to make that happen? Play around with different sales numbers for different programs to see what feels like the right fit to you.

my Amazing 2014 goals

What do you need to do to create and support a
business that earns your income goal?

Use the gifts
you have.
You were born for
a very important
reason...

my Amazing goals 2014

HOW MUCH WILL YOU EXTEND THE REACH OF YOUR BUSINESS THIS YEAR?

By the end of 2014, how big will your mailing list be?

By the end of 2014, how many of the following will you have?

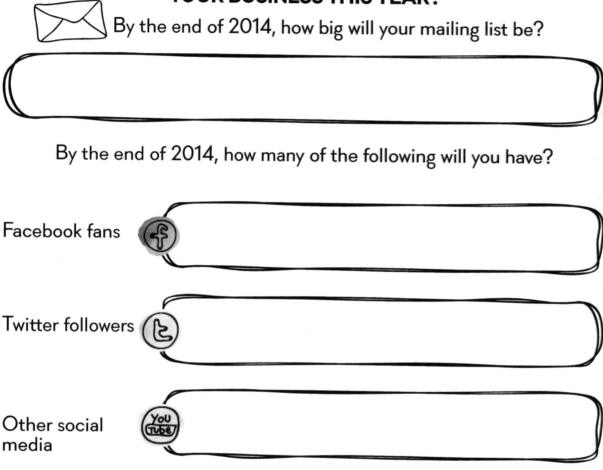

Facebook fans

Twitter followers

Other social media

Where would you like to get media mentions this year?

my Amazing goals 2014

WHAT WILL YOU CREATE THIS YEAR?

What new products/services will you create?

How many blog posts will you create this year?

How many ezines/newsletters will you send out this year?

What free opt-in offers will you create this year?

my Amazing goals 2014

Taking holidays are ridunkulously important for your mental vibrance, work/life balance and your joy for life.

How many holidays will you take this year?

When?

What do you need to do to make them happen?

What other goals do you want to make for your business this year?

Do you want to donate time or money this year?
Who do you want to help and how?

What do I need to learn about this year...

...to propel me & my business forward?

What teachers & mentors would I like to invite into my life?

NEXT STEP:
MAKE YOUR GOALS HAPPEN!

Now!

Here's the place where we are going to make the difference between us totally forgetting our goals + making our goals and dreams HAPPEN.

We need to SCHEDULE IN our goals.

For each of the goals you've written down, I want you to assign a DATE to them. Then head to the end of the workbook and start collating them into your calendar. Whether you decide to make them all match up in your online calendar as well or tattoo them as a calendar on your butt, it doesn't matter. Whatever is the style that works for YOU is the best one.

Make sure your goals are ACTIONABLE.

CHOP YOUR LARGE GOALS DOWN INTO SMALL ONES.

For example, if you've decided to write a book this year, you can chop it in to:

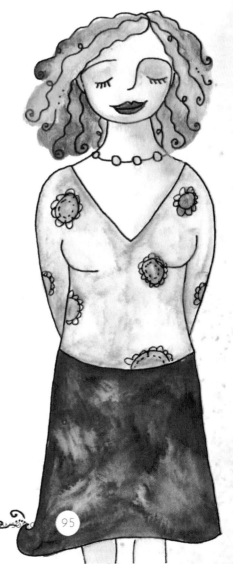

☆ chapter at a time
☆ daily word count
☆ deadline for each section
☆ and a deadline for all the book.

And (gasp!) put it in your calendar.

LEONIE'S THREE STEP SUCCESS PLAN!

1 Make everything ACTIONABLE.
2 If it feels too hard, CHOP IT DOWN.
3 And SCHEDULE IT IN.

LIFE AND BUSINESS IS A VISION QUEST.

A MEDICINE JOURNEY.

DESIGNED TO TAKE YOU TO THE HEART
OF WHO YOU ARE AND
WHAT IS POSSIBLE.

DESIGNED TO MAKE YOU HEAL.

IT'S ABOUT DEEP BRAVERY.

A LIFE GENERATED ON DEEP FAITH.

AND DEEP, ABIDING JOY.

How I Currently Spend My Biz Time

Create a pie chart of how you spend your time...

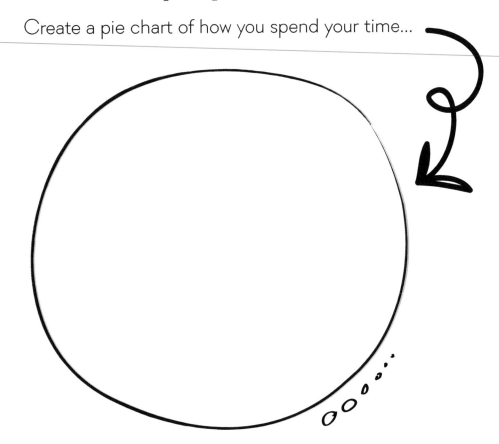

How I Want to Spend My Biz Time

CREATE A
Biz Dreamboard

I have created dreamboards for my business for years. They are powerful visual messengers of where your business is wanting to head that will keep you on track throughout the year. Every day, I work beneath my business dreamboard. I absorb my goals. And I align my actions with my intentions.

That's the power of dreamboards - to make our business dreams come true.

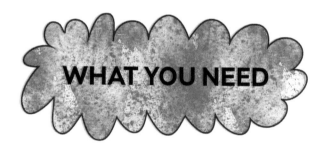

WHAT YOU NEED

 A PIECE OF CARDBOARD, THICK PAPER OR CANVAS IN WHATEVER SIZE FEELS RIGHT TO YOU.

 MAGAZINES, NEWSPAPERS, PHOTOS, IMAGES & WORDS.

 GLUE.

 A LITTLE BLEND OF OPENESS, COURAGE, JOY & A SPRINKLE OF HOPE.

 TOP WITH ESSENCE OF BIG DREAMS.

CREATE A  Dream Board FOR 2014

AND NOW...

 Search through the magazines, etc. for images & words of all the things you'd like to draw into your life experience & feel during your year.

 Choose images & words that lift you up, inspire you and make you feel radiant. Ignore all images & words that feel like a "should."

 Paste them onto your cardboard until it feels just right for your gorgeous spirit.

 Put it in a place where you can see it when you fall asleep & as you wake up.

 Watch as it is all drawn magically into your life...

PERSONAL SHARING

I wanted to share with you one of the first dreamboards I made for my business. Not only did it help propel my business into success by reminding me of my intentions, it also helped me see what my soul purpose was, and how my business was supposed to serve others.

I've gone on to create many more dreamboards for my business as I evolved and my business evolved. But this one holds a special place in my heart for giving me that total faith and clarity that this is what I was born to do. And that all I had to do was step up every single day to shine my light and help the people that I was supposed to.

Business is never about us. It's about helping the people we were born to help. We were each born with special gifts. Your job is not to worry about whether you are worthy or whether you should. Your job is simple - step up. Shine. Be the biggest light you can.

The entrepreneur's path can be the most spiritual experience of your life.

You will be called on to change every part of you that holds you back, so that you may step into your brightest magnificence.

The path of growth, of expansion,
of transformation, of change
is not always the easy one.

It will cause you to face your fears, all the parts of
you that are undeveloped.

You have no choice but to step into this, whole of
face and whole of heart.

This is the path that is calling you, the path that
has been destined for you.

This is the path that is calling your greatness out of you. It is the
path that calls you to dream your biggest dream.

WHAT DO YOU WANT TO STOP DOING THIS YEAR?

DESCRIBE YOUR DREAMIEST DAY IN BUSINESS THAT YOU WOULD ♥ LOVE ♥ TO HAPPEN THIS YEAR

PLAN YOUR PLANNING RETREAT

Planning retreats or strategy days or "business attunements" as I call them are SUCH an essential part of growing and blooming an incredible business.

You need regular time each year (sometimes multiple times a year) to realign yourself with your business attunements, make sure you are on track, correct any parts that aren't working and open yourself up to the next vision of your business growth.

For me, these retreats come as a total "energy download" (to use hippy speak). I feel buzzing with excitement as I see the next vision of where my business wants to head, how much it wants to grow to, and what I need to do to take it there. They are incredibly useful.

Handy hints for running your own:

- Work out a way for you to not work IN your business during this time - you need time away from the business so you can see the big picture. Arrange for a VA to look after your business in the meantime.

- Consider location. It's often useful to get away from your usual work location to give you a clear view.

- Consider including staff who you think are ready to step up + contribute to the vision of your business.

- You can re-use the questions from this workbook for your next retreat. They can form a great structure for business planning.

- Schedule in regular reviews of this workbook + any outcomes from your planning retreat to stay aligned with your goals + vision. I have a monthly check-in session with my Chief Operations Officer and we look over our retreat book together. I always get new insights from it!

WHEN FEELS RIGHT FOR YOUR NEXT PLANNING RETREAT?

GET YOUR BONUS 2014 CREATE YOUR AMAZING YEAR IN BUSINESS CALENDAR!

Just for being a workbook goddess, I want to give you a free matching gift... the official 2014 Create Your Amazing Year in Business calendar!

Head to: www.leoniedawson.com/2014bizbonus

to get your FREE BONUS calendar now!

YOU DID IT, YOU AMAZING SOUL!

You put in the time, energy & soul space to dream, create, cultivate, manifest & plan your amazing year in business and life.

You've set the wheels in motion for your goals to come true, your miracles to be made, your dreams to be born. Magic, goodness, love & abundance are on their way to you!

Just remember, the more you revisit this workbook, the more you become intimate with these goals of yours, the faster they will happen. Schedule your goals into your calendar and start NOW. Progress leads to more progress. By following this workbook, you're setting yourself up for increased productivity, prosperity & soul purpose.

I believe in you & your dreams. You are so needed in this world, & you are a gift to all of us.

CONGRATULATIONS AGAIN!

Now let's go make some of those amazing dreams of yours happen!

All my love + best wishes,

Want to spread the word along about this workbook & receive THANK YOU MONEYS?

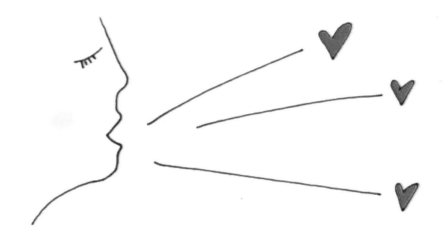

Sign up to become an affiliate (for FREE!) and receive 50% every time someone buys a workbook because of you!

You'll be helping the people who need this workbook to change their lives AND receiving some gorgeous thank you monies at the same time!

SIGN UP NOW SO WE CAN SEND YOU MOOLAH!

www.Leoniedawson.com/AMBASSADOR

what if you make

2014

your most

Amazing

year yet?

GET THE ULTIMATE AMAZING BIZ + LIFE RESOURCES!

THE BUSINESS GODDESS E-COURSE

A complete guide on how to make money online, the blueprint of how I did it. 100+ ways to market magically, mindfully & joyously, and how to stay sane & joyful when business gets rocky!

Includes bonuses of: **A Pocketfull of Business Advisors** & the **Magic Money Making Kit!**

HOW TO HIRE, GROW + KEEP A SHINING SIX FIGURE TEAM

In this guide you'll learn when to hire, who to hire, how to hire without making mistakes, how to develop + grow your team so they become truly exceptional + how to keep them. This guide will help you create an amazing team, supercharge your business growth + bring you so much more joy, love + support into your life.

Join the Academy + get everything you need at an amazing price!
www.amazingbizandlifeacademy.com

RADIANT GODDESS E-COURSE

A 21-day nutrition, movement & meditation journey to revitalise your body, mind & soul! You'll be guided by gorgeous menu plans, movement plans, spirit + inspiration projects, and meditations to guide you as you reawaken your Radiant Goddess self. This is perfect if you're ready to be moving, meditating, eating & discovering in a joyful, spirited goddess way. Ready to feel blissed out, inspired & radiant?

CREATIVE GODDESS E-COURSE

A six-week guided journey to discover the Creative Goddess in you! This e-course is both practical + spiritual, and will help you discover (or remember!) that you were born an artist, art can help you heal, creativity can make your spirituality bloom in new & beautiful ways, and that you really are a creative goddess. If you're ready to remember how inspired, wise & courageous you are, this journey is for you!

Join the Academy + get everything you need at an amazing price!
www.amazingbizandlifeacademy.com

CREATE YOUR GODDESS HAVEN E-COURSE

6 weeks to creating your decluttered, sacred, nourishing haven! Are you ready to get more productive, peaceful + organised? Are you ready to clear negative, draining energy out of your space + attract more good things? Join the Create Your Goddess Haven e-course and transform your home + office into an organised, energetically cleansed, feng-shui-sorted + good-things-attracting haven!

BEST DAY EVER MEDITATION

Start your day off right with this short, powerful meditation that will help you be:

- happier
- more productive
- crazy inspired

Join the Academy + get everything you need at an amazing price!
www.amazingbizandlifeacademy.com

DIVINE DREAMING
MEDITATION KIT

A meditation kit to help you get to sleep easier & have more divine dreams. This meditation will help you drift into slumber more easily, have wise + healing dreams, feel more revitalised when you awaken & have way more glorious days because your nights are so much more nourishing!

RELEASING FEARS
MEDITATION KIT

Use this meditation to let go, be free, and shine. This meditation is powerful for whenever you're feeling stuck, lost or down from any old pains and fears you may have. You'll feel less stuck by your fears, stronger and clearer, and so much freer to chase your big, beautiful dreams!

CHAKRA HEALING
MEDITATION KIT

Are you feeling depleted, and in need of energy? Do you want to activate spiritual, physical and emotional healing all over your body? Are you ready to experience the powerful practice of chakra healing? This meditation will guide you into a magical experience that will leave you feeling supported, inspired and joyful. A truly sacred experience.

Join the Academy + get everything you need at an amazing price!
www.amazingbizandlifeacademy.com

HOLY DINGER
UBER DEEP
ZENNIFYING
MEDITATION KIT

Are your fears holding you back? This meditation kit will help you let go of your fears & give you the courage to move forward.

SACRED SPACE
CLEARING KIT

Having a home that is energetically cleansed & clear is incredibly important for you + your family's happiness, sense of peace + productivity. This kit will power you with all the tools you need to make your home + office shine + help you feel reinvigorated, peaceful, productive + happy.

CREATING WITH KIDS
WORKSHOP

We mamas, we need our art. And we need to include our kids in it too. And it's different from ABF (Art Before Kids). It takes a whole new level of art skills, tools, perspectives & set-up. So Ostara & I decided to invite you around... to paint with us, to spill water & eat paint & laugh wildly & get rained on... and find out what it is to be CREATIVE MAMA GODDESSES.

Join the Academy + get everything you need at an amazing price!
www.amazingbizandlifeacademy.com

Want it all?

Get the complete AMAZING BIZ + LIFE package and
for a crazy generous price too!

Join the AMAZING BIZ + LIFE ACADEMY
+ get over $3500 of my programs (including
BOTH of next years' workbooks!) for just $497
(& payment plans are available too!)

Get the complete AMAZING BIZ + LIFE ACADEMY
now & make 2014 truly amazing!

Join the Academy + get everything you need at an amazing price!
www.amazingbizandlifeacademy.com

Made in the USA
Lexington, KY
31 December 2013